Colours
and
Shapes

illustrated by Mark Airs

Everything has a colour. Some things have many colours.

Things we play with have colours.

Things we eat have colours.

Things in our homes have colours.

Things in the street have colours.

What colours are you wearing today?

red

red car

red apple

red mug

red ladybird

blue

blue hat

blue blocks

blue ball

blue bird

Have fun together seeing how many different shades of blue you can find. How many blue things can you find as you count to ten?

yellow

yellow banana

yellow duck

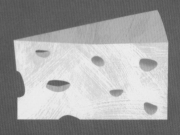

yellow sun

yellow cheese

green

green T-shirt

green leaf

green watering can

green frog

When you are in the garden or park, look for different shades of green. Use words like 'light', 'pale' and 'dark' to describe them.

purple

purple grapes

purple trousers

purple pencils

purple flowers

orange

orange carrot

orange fish

orange butterfly

orange digger

brown

brown puppy

brown teddy

brown rabbit

brown boots

black

black helicopter

black horse

black jumper

black cat

Which toys are the same colour?

Can you sort your own toys into groups of colours?

Look at all the colours on the train!

What colour is the funnel?
What colour is the roof?

Mixing paints is good fun.

red

blue

purple

Red and blue make purple.

red

yellow

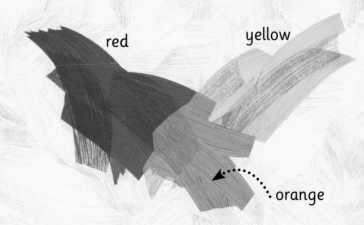

orange

Red and yellow make orange.

orange

red

yellow

purple

green

blue

·········· brown

Red, blue and yellow make brown.

circle

Everything around us has a shape.

This is a circle.

What colour is the circle?

Trace round each circle with your finger.

triangle

This is a triangle.

It has three corners.

Can you point to all three corners?

How many triangles can you see here?

sail

pizza

cheese

party hat

square

This is a square.

It has four sides all the same.

Trace the square with your finger.

Many things are square-shaped.

window

puzzle

painting

game board

rectangle

This is a rectangle.

It has two long sides and two short sides.

Talk to your child about the differences between a rectangle (two sides long and two sides short) and a square (all sides the same length).

Can you find these rectangles in your house?

brick

book

pencil case

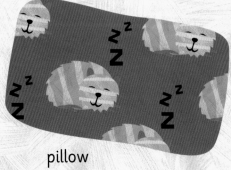

pillow

A feast of colours and shapes, what a treat!
Say the names of the shapes you would eat.